Silent Cries

TEARS IN THE DARK LEFT UNSPOKEN

Silent Cries

THE PAIN THAT PRODUCED YOUR TEARS IS BIRTHING YOUR PURPOSE

GLINDA L. BROCK

Published by Publish Your Gift®
An imprint of Purposely Created Publishing Group, LLC

Printed in the United States of America

ISBN: 978-1-64484-520-2 (print)
ISBN: 978-1-64484-521-9 (ebook)

This book is dedicated to all the hearts of the world. May these words enter in and give hope to the hopeless and bring light to any darkness. I dedicate this book to everyone who has been a light for me and others. To my children, Amarion and Nehemiah, may you both be all that God has called you to be! May the greatness that is yet to be seen in this world take root and sprout forth like a weed in the garden, until it overtakes that which we thought was beautiful, and then becomes the most desired among all the earth. Often the weed appears to be beautiful until we experience the blossoming of a fragrant rose.

Table of Contents

Introduction

Dear Lord,

Let my fingers tell a story that my heart just can't express…

As my heart overflows down into my finger-tips, allow them to translate every emotion and every passionate word precisely to all who will read them.

Today is a day of truth, the truth that lies deep within my soul. Everyone has a truth, something that they sometimes keep to themselves and share just with our Heavenly Father. Well, here is mine. I pray that with every word someone is touched and made whole. I pray that these words bring peace to someone's troubled heart and mind. I pray that someone's soul will be delivered and set free. For if the Son sets you free you are free indeed. I pray that this helps bring love back into the heart of many and that someone is able to find their way back to God and back to everything that He is, for He is waiting. I pray that my voice helps someone regain theirs and that this is read in its entirety, so someone's joy may be restored and someone's life changed, so they can give God all the glory and all the praise that is due His glorious name.

There is no better time than the present to make things right and no better time than the present to get up from a place of destruction. Someone's destruction may be depression and anxiety, and another person's may be their thoughts and actions. There is someone reading this who has no peace, no joy, no hope, or who may have thoughts of suicide. Whatever the thing is that wants to destroy you and your purpose, know that it is the work of iniquity and the works of Satan. His only plan is to steal, kill, and destroy. His plan is to cause you, by any means necessary, to be anything but what God has already called you to be from your mother's womb! You were placed here at this very moment in time for a purpose that God has designed and that must come to pass. Satan's job is to blind you and attempt to throw you off course and cause you to think the opposite of what God has already predestined for your life. Well, I am so glad that our Heavenly Father is forever waiting with open arms, and the time is now to get in His presence. It is time to once again speak those things that are of God and break free from all that has you bound.

This is my journey, dear Lord, and this is Your glory...

It is all for You, my King, all for your glory. I am nothing but a speck of dust that was spoken into something more. Whatever I do and whatever I say must be pleasing to You, dear Lord. Take out of me anything that is not of You and replace it with everything that is of You, my King. Let there be no sign of me and only let You remain.

I must do whatever it takes to please You and bring fame to Your magnificent name, for all the glory and victory belong to You my Heavenly Father.

Thank You for choosing me, I will rejoice!

Help me be strong, and keep the faith. Strengthen me, dear Lord, and heal every wound. Allow these words to bring life to the deepest hurt and open the most guarded heart.

I am Yours, my Master. Here I am. Use me as You please. Empty me out and shine brighter than ever before through me, dear Lord. It is for this purpose that I was created and for this moment that I was brought into existence. You are my everything, my God, and without You I am absolutely lost and absolutely nothing. I need You more than anything. You are my bread of life, my breath of fresh air, my Rose of Sharon, my deliverer, my void filler, my provider, my way maker, my healer. You are my mother, my father, my strength, my joy, my peace, my King of kings, and my Lord of lords, my everything. You are my God!

CHAPTER 1

My Heart Unfolded

I've learned that I am just a million and one plus a billion and one broken pieces that need putting back together. But how? For how can you fix a glass that has been completely shattered into dust, its original form? You can't. For it is forever tossed and swept into the trash, never to be thought of again. Then, it is easily replaced with a replica. So, tell me how do I mend all these broken pieces, and how do I avoid being so broken that I am no longer tossed and swept away never to be remembered again? Or am I already forgotten, never to be remembered, never to be thought of again? Do I even exist? Am I even here? Am I real? Am I even alive? Or am I already the dust, back to my original state?

Sometimes, it's so hard for me to express exactly how I feel. The only thing that comes close is letting this pen unite with this paper or the using of the keys on my keyboard to type the words that I could not always utter from my lips. The best word to express this feeling of anxiety, stress, pressure, loneliness, hurt, and pain is "indescribable." These are emotions that can only be felt, so you understand what it is to be me in such moments in my life, moments that have forced me into a place far greater than anything that I could ever imagine. My heart is forever overflowing with emotion from somewhere far deeper than any one word could ever explain.

What do you do when you feel like God has forgotten all about you?

There were times in my life when I questioned whether God was there. Did He care about me or the debacles that were going on in my life at different times? I even remember asking myself, "If He is present then why doesn't He do something about all the things that are going on that I have no control over that are causing havoc in my life?" All it takes is a wave of His hand or a soft-spoken word, and all of the great and vast universe must obey. I wondered sometimes in tears and sometimes in anger, "Why won't He wave His hand for me or speak to the universe and make it behave?" I've tried, but it doesn't seem to be working. I remember thinking that I must be doing something wrong, and if that was the case, what must I do to get my life out of this disarray and back into alignment with whatever path God has predestined for me all for His glory?

There were times I found myself being overwhelmed with the different struggles in my life. I also realized at times I was slacking on my time with God. I used to talk with Him in the mornings, evenings, at night, or just whenever.

Then later I remember making excuses and saying to myself that I was too tired or I didn't have time. There was so much going on, and my life was so hectic that I couldn't manage to find the time to pray or commune with God. I didn't realize at the time what effect this was actually having on my entire life—spiritually, mentally, and naturally. However, I must admit that I was tremendously wrong for thinking that I could get by without connecting with God due to life's perilous situations and obstacles that were taking place.

Some of My Feelings at Certain Moments

So many feelings were tangled up within me.

I don't know what to do; my heart hurts, and feels so lonely. I feel like there is no one here, and that leaves me wondering and asking, "What do I do now?" O God, why do You seem so far away? I need You close! I need You near! So much chaos! It's just me and my children; we are so alone here! Why can't any of our prayers be answered? What is it like to feel real love and happiness? What does it feel like for someone to truly love and care about me? I feel like crying sometimes because I don't know any other way to express this overflow of emotions. It is an intense feeling of worthlessness and emptiness, and I feel like I am not loved, not wanted, and not needed by anyone for any purpose at all. I feel like busting out sometimes, but there is nothing for me to bust out of. I feel like running sometimes, but there is no place to run to. I feel like screaming sometimes, but there is no octave sharp enough that could ever begin to express the way I really feel deep within my heart and mind. I feel like I have been forgotten a long time ago, never to be remembered anymore! Sometimes, I don't know what to do with my countless thoughts and feelings other than to write them down in hopes of using this paper and pen to make some sense of what my heart is attempting to convey. There were times I felt as though my heart was bleeding from lack of love and care. I became uncertain about how much longer I had before it would die. Sometimes, it seems that the days aren't fairly given to me. I am so tired of crying, but the tears can't help but fall from my eyes which sometimes seems to be a never-ending, overflowing river.

There was a time that I felt like such a horrible person because of some of the rash decisions that I made out of chaos, hurt, and pain during my past. I wondered at times if I was truly forgiven or could have been forgiven even though we have all fallen short of His glory. Some questions that entered my mind were, "Am I truly a child of the King, and have all my sins been forgiven?" Then they were followed by these thoughts: "Maybe I don't deserve to be forgiven. Maybe this is why I don't deserve happiness. Maybe happiness doesn't want to be a part of me. Maybe I am at the point of no return."

I didn't realize it at the time, but I eventually learned that those thoughts were the thoughts of the enemy, wanting me to believe his lies. He continuously spews out lies into every vessel that will accept and soak them up because they don't know the truth.

I've been so hurt. My soul is pouring out, and I didn't want this light in me to cease to exist. I felt it breaking away and slowly letting in some darkness. I didn't want the darkness to consume me, but I found myself becoming more and more like so many others. There were people in my life who said they loved me, but they haven't shown me that. There were some who even disrespected me, lied on me, lied to me, treated me horribly, and hated me without a cause. How do I fix this? How do I kill this thing that wants to take over me? How do I defeat this? Those pills for anxiety weren't working. I was starting to hate myself for any hurt or pain I caused others, in spite of what was done to me. I should have tried harder to show the light of Christ in me. Can you forgive me? God, can you forgive me, please?

(As I dealt with some of these frustrations, I wrote this as one of many letters to God.)

A Cry from My Heart

Will You love me? I've heard there's no greater thing! I love You, and I just want You to love me back. I thought that You would love me only if I did the things that You liked. I longed for You; will You ever long for me? I want to see You; will You ever be a part of me? I need You. Is there anything that You need from me? I love to hear You; can You please whisper a little louder in my ear? I want to know You like You know me. I want to see me like You see me. I want to love me like You love me. Will You ever give up on me? Will You ever leave me? Will You ever need me like I need You? Lord, I'm searching. I'm hoping, and I'm praying for your warm embrace. I need You more than anything! I need You like my lungs need the air! Will You breathe through me and let people see You instead of me? Will You talk for me and let them hear You instead of me? Will You give me the eyes I need to clearly see what You need me to see? Will You love me? For I've heard there's no greater thing!

Knowing When I Said Yes to God

This is what I said yes to. This is God having His way. This is God doing as He pleases with me.

I just need to be still and let God have His way. Be still and let God be God! Be still and stand on the word of the Lord!

God has all power! He is great and mighty! He is Alpha and Omega, the Author and Finisher of my faith!

What do you do when your world crumbles? I had to learn how to pick up the pieces because some of the best things in life are made from scratch. God, I guess this is Your way of tearing me down, so that You can make me over to be everything You need me to be for Your glory. I wondered if I was doing something wrong, but then I heard my Heavenly Father say, "No, my child. I need you to be a witness."

I learned that in my "going through" there is a purpose! All purposes lead to God! I also believe that when I was formed in my mother's womb, God instilled everything in me I needed to go through this journey of life. I also believe that while He was forming me, every moment I said yes. I said yes to whatever He wanted of me, I said yes to everything God had in store for my life. I accepted, agreed, and was willing to surrender to Him, allowing Him to be in control and guide me through every moment of my personal journey.

To endure is to go through; to go through brings understanding. There was an awakening that was happening spiritually and a transformation that reached down deep within me. This was being done to take me to a place of staying in God's presence more, back to my source and back to the beginning. I must trust God with everything in me. Help me, Father, to do what is right at all times and to always make the decisions that are best for my life. I must be still and listen to Your voice. I know that as long as I do what You say, I'm doing what's right. I must speak when You say speak. I must be silent when You say be silent. I must move when You say move. Let your directions, my Lord, be my directions.

It is time; a new me must emerge. If this is God's will, then it must be done. If this is God's way, then it must be done this way. Everything has to align with what God says must be and must come forth. Even though my flesh is hurting and desperately crying out for relief, if this is what God has ordained, then this is what it shall be. For in the end, it is all working together for my good. Therefore, it must be, so that God can be glorified! It's not about me. It's all about God!

Touch me, Lord, ever so gently, like only You can! Teach me all things! Dear Lord, change everything about me into Your likeness!

As these teardrops continue to roll down my face in what seems to be a never-ending flow, I know nothing else but to hold onto You, as You hold onto me.

Thank You, Heavenly Father, for Your sweet, gentle kiss upon my forehead, saying, "Daughter, I am here." You calm my spirit. I need that most right now.

CHAPTER 2

For a Purpose, God's Purpose

Sometimes, there is an undeniable pressing in my spirit to do things that undoubtedly must be done to carry out God's plan. Whatever His plans are is the purpose that He has for our lives. Therefore, I must do those things that He places within my spirit to do. These are the necessary things because if He gives it to you to do, then it must be done to fulfill your purpose for your life for His glory.

However, at times I have been hesitant. My hesitation came from not being sure of who I was in God or what my purpose was. As a result, I listened to what the enemy said about me when I should only have listened to the voice of the

Lord. I should trust Him completely to do in me whatever He desires.

Do in me what you will, dear Lord
Take out of me what you will, I say
Do it now please, right away
Forever lead me, dear Lord
Help show me the way
For your timing is always perfect
So, I must do as You say
Take out of me what You must, right away
I need You more and more each day
Give me a heart like Yours, dear Lord

Give me a mind like Yours, I pray.

There is a forever burning flame inside of me that burns with the intensity of the sun. There is a passion deep within me that burns like fresh fire straight from the heavens. There is a love deep down within me that is as vast as all of God's universe. There is something much greater than all of this, and it overtakes my soul and consumes me whole until I am no longer me in the flesh but me in spirit and in truth and the very essence of what God wants me to be. I am fully committed to Him, fully focused on Him, fully wrapped in Him, fully anchored in Him!

The question is, "Why can't I remain this way?" My only explanation is that it must be due to life's trials and tribulations. It causes me to think like a person in my human, natural state rather than a spirit connected with God.

Sometimes, I feel like hiding from the world, hiding from everything. Hiding from all troubles, all problems, all stresses, all anxieties, and everything that has me bound. I need to be free of it all. Set me free my Heavenly Father.

In times such as this, I know God wants us to trust Him and know that His ways are always perfect! It is not our job to know God's plan but to trust His plan is His perfect will for our lives.

So often I have questioned certain situations in my life. Looking back, I know that not all of them were because of what God said must be. However, some things were a result of me not being in Him fully and not allowing Him to have His way in my life. Some of those situations were because of decisions that I made without consulting God and not getting the necessary guidance for my life. Therefore, Lord, I have learned, and I yield to You and give You total control, Heavenly Father. Have Your way! Also, I know that God puts you in places where He needs you to be at that moment. I want to remain connected in order to stay only in the places God wants me to be and to make the decisions God desires for me to make. I desire to passionately follow and obey.

I believe greater faith in God leads to greater blessings! Faith can cause God to move on your behalf. However, you must realize, as I am still learning, just because God hasn't moved that situation just yet doesn't mean that He didn't hear you. It also doesn't mean that He won't do it. Oh, He is going to do everything that He promised! If He said it, so shall it be! There is a time and a season for everything. Just wait on Him and know that everything that He has spoken must come to pass! In the midst of this, I can see that the devil is attempting to attack those areas of weakness in me. I forever cast out whatever the enemy has attempted to plant within me and welcome all that God has for me! Strengthen me, dear Lord, in every area of my life. There were times when the devil was trying to devour me. But I belong to God, and I must trust that He will give me all the strength I need to go through whatever it is I must endure, for His glory.

I remember someone saying that God is going to require of you the very thing that you love the most, the thing that you hold dear! He is going to ask that of you. Well, Lord, here I am, broken... I am Yours, use me as You please.

This is the moment; this is the hour!

I must keep pressing. I have no other choice because giving up and throwing in the towel is not an option! I must keep trusting in the Lord and believe with everything in me that it is already done! We all must believe and be strong in the Lord and the power of His might! (Ephesians 6:10-18).

CHAPTER 3

A Faint Voice in the Wilderness

That delightful, blissful moment when I think I have found that little niche or thing that makes me feel a part of the family, something seems to always come along and remind me otherwise. Something seems to always bring me back to the tangible things that are present before me, both those vividly seen with the eyes and those undeniably felt by my now fainting heart. Maybe it's just the gravity that surrounds me. Yes, it happens every time; I can never get too far gone. I believe it has a duty to keep me grounded each time I drift away above the clouds. It always seems to bring me back down to the ground and to the truth of my reality again.

When it seems like no one cares and you are all alone, God is always there. When it seems like you have nowhere to go and nowhere to turn, God is still there. He sees every teardrop and hears every cry. Pray to our Heavenly Father and cry out to Him. It's okay to cry, but when you cry, cry Jesus! Call on His name. Then you shall rejoice because those tears of sorrow will turn into tears of joy! Keep praying because indeed the effectual, fervent prayers of a righteous man availeth much (James 5:16).

There were times in my life when I felt all alone. There were countless times when I felt like no one cared. It seemed as though there was no one I could run to or nowhere to run. Then as the tears started to flow, I felt God speaking to my heart. I asked for more of God, and I prayed that He would manifest Himself in me, so that I could see Him in a mighty, miraculous way in my life. The great I AM is forever present. He used every moment that the devil meant to destroy me and tear me down to build me up and to let me know that He was in control because every struggle, every fight was already won. God has all power and all victory!

I've learned that in the middle of going through a problem, it can bring about many different mixed emotions. This may leave you feeling lost, hopeless, afraid, and even unwanted, unloved, empty, or misunderstood at times. I have also come to the realization that this is why I must always stay before the King and in His presence. How can you truly know God for yourself if you have never experienced Him for yourself? We must always know that God is with us, and what the devil meant for evil God will turn it around for our good. It has a purpose for your life, a purpose to glorify God! Have faith in God! God is the only way! God is the answer! We must always pray and seek His face continuously.

"Trust in the Lord with all thine heart; and lean not unto thine own understanding. In all thy ways acknowledge him, and he shall direct thy paths" (Proverbs 3:5-7).

The living word states, "The Lord hath appeared of old unto me, saying, Yea, I have loved thee with an everlasting love: therefore, with lovingkindness have I drawn thee" (Jeremiah 31:3).

As God beckoned me, I drew nearer and welcomed Him into my life. I allowed God to dwell within me and to take total control. I want to always move into a deeper connection with our Heavenly Father. I pray that God will always keep my mind, heart, body, and spirit pure, so that I will continue to worship Him in spirit and in truth. For what is in a moment? It is the opportunity to reverence God for who He is and praise Him with everything in you!

I feel as though there are sometimes not enough words that could ever be spoken, no matter how sweet they may sound, or enough tears I could ever cry, nor enough prayers that I could ever pray to make things be what I want them to be. Sometimes, I'm not ready for my day to begin, and other days, I'm not ready for it to end. I've had many sleepless nights, but I thank God when He brings peace and comfort!

For, now is the time! Now is the hour. Greater is coming, Greater is here! Thank You, Lord, for Your greatness! Thank You, Lord, for who You are! Glory to Your name! I am never alone. Forever grace me with Your presence, dear Lord! However You do it Lord, allow Your spirit and anointing to overflow within me...

CHAPTER 4

The Hidden Gem

A gem is a rare and special treasure, and if ever found, it has become the most desired by all who have gained new knowledge of its proven existence. We are the gem, and we are very special. We have abilities to do great and awesome things by the power that dwells within us, far beyond what we can perceive with any current thought or idea. However, we are very capable of doing that and much more. A lot of times we don't know that we are carrying something so special and desired and needed in this world. We have so much greatness in us, and for the most part, it is lying dormant and needs to be awakened. That great awesome thing that lies within is so deeply desired by the world, and once it is revealed (proven existence), it is even more desired.

I've come to realize that not everyone is going to like you or even show you the genuine love and care you are searching or longing for. You must continue to pray and build a relationship with God, so others' negative opinions of you no longer matter as long as you are staying in God's will. I could no longer make excuses or allow the outside negativity to seep in. I also must guard the gates of my heart. There came a point when I had to stop viewing myself as a victim and start acknowledging myself as victorious. It's all about guarding your heart, mind, and spirit. Start thinking those things that are of God and stop thinking those things that will keep you limited. Aim to concentrate on the great things God still has in store for you and what you must do for God. Pray about your purpose and start walking in it as God directs you every step of the way. I've learned to continue to pray about what to do. God's ways are not like ours, and His timing is always perfect. I am still working on this. Sometimes, I have been so quick to do something without first consulting God. I am still working on making sure that whatever I do and whatever I speak is pleasing to the Lord. I want His will to be done in my life because I want the best of the best of the very, very best and nothing less! (Laughing out loud) It's all about serving God and operating in your divine purpose that is pre-destined for your life!

All negative thoughts must go! All negative people must go! All negative actions must cease now! This life as we know it in the natural form is too short and must not be taken for granted. There is another life that we must embrace one day as so many before us who have transitioned to their final and ultimate destination have. We must do what is right and repent from those things that are not like God to have eternal life in Heaven, the place that God intended for us. What things are keeping you from serving God or from operating in your divine purpose?

There are people who appear to be so happy and jolly. They are laughing and joking and just enjoying themselves. The same people may look at me smiling and laughing but have no idea what it takes sometimes for a smile to emerge on my face. There is a story to be told behind the smile, behind the laughter, and the mask of luxury. What sometimes may look glamorous or enticing may be the complete opposite inside the actual dwellings of an individual's mind and spirit.

Sometimes, there is pain that lies deep within that must be plucked out. Therefore, we must go deeper than the surface and get to the very core. You have waited far too long; deliverance and healing are needed. Everyone who is hurting wants the pain to end, but everyone is not aware of a remedy. Keep smiling and keep fighting. God is the remedy. I have learned that it is hard to smile under stress. If one is depressed or dealing with issues that are overwhelming and frustrating, smiling can seem to be nearly impossible. But through Christ, all things are possible. I have learned if I can muster up enough in me to smile, then I am still in the fight. I have not thrown in the towel, and I have not given up. When the devil thinks that he has stolen your joy, fight and smile as you think of the goodness of the Lord. When he starts telling you lies and trying to destroy something that God has already said must be, smile. You are smiling because you have already won; every battle has already been fought, and the enemy is already defeated. In the midst of pain, some people resort to different tactics, hoping to ease their agony. Some people start overeating or not eating at all, drinking, using drugs, or engaging in whatever thing the enemy brings before them. They are trying to recreate any moment of peace that they can recollect and are trying so desperately to kill whatever pain is present. They soon realize that it only masked the pain for a moment, and then they repeat the routine as often as they need to for some relief. Well, God is the answer because He is love, and He is merciful. Great and mighty is our God!

To those of you who are hurting know that Philippians 4:7-9 states:

"And the peace of God, which passeth all understanding, shall keep your hearts and minds through Christ Jesus. Finally, brethren, whatsoever things are true, whatsoever things are honest, whatsoever things are just, whatsoever things are pure, whatsoever things are lovely, whatsoever things are of good report; if there be any virtue, and if there be any praise, think on these things. Those things, which ye have both learned, and received, and heard, and seen in me, do: and the God of peace shall be with you."

The trials and tribulations that you are encountering are coming to be in your life at those moments that God has already predestined, as long as you are staying in His will. Sometimes, we can bring things on ourselves when we step out of the will of God but being in His will ensures that no matter what comes your way, you are still on the right path.

Despite being hurt and broken, misused and abused, I must have no excuse for not serving the Lord. Let's start helping one another in a way that uplifts and rebuilds. Empty out what God has placed in you to give as a service to somebody that is in need. God is soon to return, and He is coming back for His people. Will He find you giving unto that which brings Him glory, or will He find you going deeper into the grasp of the enemy? Some things we must all ask ourselves.

If you have never been hurt before, how would you know for yourself that God is a healer? If you have never been broken, how would you know for yourself it is God that restores? If you have never been misused and abused, how would you know for yourself that God is a deliverer that can and will meet you at the point of your need? Whatever it is, God is always the answer.

The hidden gem lies within each of us as we emerge from the dust of our past selves and come into the newness of what God has been graciously and particularly molding us into. Everything that you have gone through, everything that you have endured, every trial, and every teardrop are there to help the hidden gem that you are, hidden away in a dark place, come to the light. Let the gem in you come out and shine through for it is desired and needed.

CHAPTER 5

Secret Struggles

Early one morning as I looked out the window, I saw a true reflection of myself that shined brightly from the glass. For some reason, I seemed to have missed something while looking in the mirror that could have only been seen as a true reflection of myself as I looked out the window with all the curtains pulled back. When looking in the mirror, you are getting yourself prepared for your day. You may be doing your hair or makeup, or you may even be checking out the outfit that you are wearing to see if it is the right one for the occasion. But when you are looking out the window, you aren't looking to glamorize yourself. You are looking to view the world outside, and sometimes, you just happen to catch a glimpse of yourself, your true self. Are you standing or sitting with a straight face or a smile? Do you have a frown or show some sadness? What is your reflection showing? The mirror had only shown me what I wanted to see, and I was easily able to fix any imperfections with a little bit of foundation or mask it somehow with a man-made substance. But the reflection showed me the things that I hid and wanted to stay hidden so deeply within. That's when those secret struggles began to surface, and I had to acknowledge that they existed and completely armor up, so I could confront them. First, I had to prepare myself for what was about to unfold within me. Was I ready to know all that I had hidden away in the deep parts of me that was so carefully placed away? On the surface lies one thing, but what is it that I was about to reveal within myself? I started to pray about this because I wasn't sure if I was completely ready to uncover the things that I had locked away that were never dealt with.

Where oh where should I begin? Let's see. Yes, I will start here…

One thing my reflection showed me was that I still had some "feeling alone" issues that I had to deal with. I am usually smiling or joining in with laughter at the appropriate times. I am usually showing love and always ready to embrace someone with a warm, loving hug. However, there was always a deep longing and a desire for something more that grew tremendously every waking moment. I still felt empty and incomplete at times. No matter how much love I thought I was pouring out, I just wasn't getting everything I needed. I pushed those feelings away. Sometimes, it's nothing that one person can give. Sometimes, they may have been giving all they had to give emotionally, but my heart still longed for much more than I even understood. My spirit still yearned for so much. There were some missing pieces that I lost or never had that were needed in order to complete the puzzle. My heart had some holes in it that needed some plugs the size of Jesus to fix them. Sometimes, I would toss and turn, not able to go to sleep and not even sure if I was ready to fall asleep.

My thoughts wandered, not knowing what the day ahead would look like. Would I be feeling the same anguish, and if so, what could be done to feel the very opposite? Erase the emptiness. O dear Lord, grow some new life where there is nothing present.

One extremely large hole I had was for my children because I felt as though I had failed them in so many ways. God gave me the guardianship and charge of birthing and mothering two of His kings, and ideally, they should have a father present in their lives to help show them and groom them to be proper and respectable young men. As the story goes, things just didn't turn out that way. So, here I am raising my two young men, and they have no male figure to help guide them into manhood. I am now, for the first time, willing to say that I can't teach them to be men. I always knew that, but I never wanted to admit it to myself. I feared if I did, it would make me feel vulnerable and that I failed them as their mother. Unfortunately, as life would have it, things just didn't turn out as planned. There were many times I just wasn't ready to face that reality, so I always shoved it away every time the thought entered my mind. I swiftly replaced it with something else. I apologize to both of you, my handsome, young men of God. I pray that God redeems the time, and your voids are completely filled, and you both are forever blessed and covered with God's love and grace.

I had another hole within me that seemed to grow bigger and deeper. This hole was there for my family because I always wanted us to have a better connection and be able to really have that unbreakable bond and closeness that family should share. Well, I know that I'm not alone in this even though it feels like I am.

Another thing that my reflection showed me was that I had a lot of guilt for lost time. Time is so precious and valuable. However, I wasted so much time that I could have used to do so much more for God, unlocking all the greatness within that would allow me to soar to higher heights and greater manifestations that were still waiting to be birthed. I realized that my unawareness and previous life now had me racing to make up for lost time. At one point, I was even unaware that I was not using my five senses to their full capabilities. I was blinded by what was in front of me. The obstacles blocked my view, and my mind believed the illusions and mirages that lay before me. Wow! I chuckle because I now realize that they didn't lay gracefully before me, they "lied" before me... And I believed the lies at times.

The Same Day of the Year

If only I could erase the date from the calendar, skip over it somehow, or sleep through it even. Yes, if only it were that simple. However, life isn't always so simple. Sometimes, the complexity of it all knows no end. Life only knows that another second must come forth until God says no more. Moment by moment, second by second, minute by minute, hour by hour, day by day, week by week, month by month, and year by year, until God says no more. It is the day that the Lord has made; I shall rejoice and be glad in it. Yet, I am so torn and broken; I have so much heartache. I wish I could disappear for just twenty-four hours and then come back. I wish I could maybe dwell in another place, in another time for just twenty-four hours if it were possible and then come back. I'd love to be in another place, a place where love existed, a place where my heart had no cracks or broken pieces, a place where I belonged, a place where my children felt free and welcomed for just twenty-four hours, possibly never wanting to return. Where is this place of splendor, which I have never laid eyes upon? What are your coordinates? How do I locate you? Does Google Maps know the way? Or do I need a plane ticket to travel? If only I could close my eyes and pray that God would take me there in my dreams. This place of splendor, this place of so much love, peace, great joy, and happiness. Yes, this is the place where I belong, within the magnificent wonder of lifted burdens where all freedom abides.

God said that He is my burden bearer, and He is the lifter of my head. He is always there with me right there in the midst. All I must do is keep calling on Him until the atmosphere around me changes. Once it gets a whiff of Jesus, something will happen. Things cannot remain the same.

There were many times I felt so all alone and completely empty. I struggled with a sense of belonging and feelings of having no real value. I was in need of something to revive me. I needed something to give life to my spirit. I needed to grasp hold of something that would keep me from losing my mind each day. I was in need of something that would hold me up when I was down and something that would carry me when I couldn't walk and something that would talk for me when my mind seemed like it was on autopilot, speaking words but not really knowing what was going on around me or what I was even speaking. I needed something that would let me know that I was in fact something and not just a speck of matter taking up space. I needed something that would speak to everything that was in me, on me, around me, over me, and close to me and tell it that I was something more. I needed to know that I was created with an absolute purpose that existed because the God of gods and Lord of lords called me forth. The great I AM called me to be. This is what I needed to know. Who I am had to be awakened and come forth.

It took some things and some events to wake up my extra sense, which goes beyond what is natural and is not easily recognizable. By this, I mean the supernatural awareness, being able to see in the dark, being able to hear what the silence was saying, is saying, and will say, being able to smell beyond what the nose will naturally recognize, being able to taste the unseasoned thing that knows no flavor, and being able to touch and feel beneath the surface and know what it is that the core knew and possessed. What does the core hold within its grasp, and can you now grasp that which is beyond the core? What is in the depths of the heart of your situations, circumstances, and distresses? What is the root cause of it, and are you able to now reach past that and give birth to the greatness that is to come? Sometimes, we may be our own problem.

Sometimes, we need to look at ourselves and allow God to fix what is not right within us, so we can truly blossom and truly flourish for now and forevermore. For out of me, I shall birth generation after generation that shall be a great legacy of divine greatness where the source of it all is our God.

Once my transformation took place, it no longer mattered that I was once empty and unaware of my true identity. It only mattered that I now knew who I was and who I belonged to. My true self is all that mattered. It was as if I was hidden somewhere in the depths of darkness or locked away somewhere far away into the vast unknown of another world within a world... Until I was awakened.

It's like being in a crowded room full of people yet no one even knows that you're there. You are screaming at the very top of your lungs, and no one hears you. "Help Meeeeeeee! Someone help me please," you shout over and over again, but no one even looks your way. You scream and scream until one day you lose your voice, and when you try to scream, there is no sound left. You then begin to reach out in hopes that someone would see your shaky fragile hands, but no one notices a thing. You can't move because it is as if you are chained to the floor without a key. Then one day with no voice left to scream for help and now so much numbness in your arms and hands for reaching out, and because you are chained to a floor that you have no key for your body has grown so weak and tired from the stress and depression and anxiety, the shame, embarrassment, even self-torment, that the only things that were able to enter in were things that disagreed with your body and spirit. They disagreed because they were not the fruits of the Spirit but the fruits of the flesh that the enemy had planted. You began to eat whatever the enemy fed you because you thought that was all you were worth. No one heard you, and no one saw you shouting and screaming for help, so you thought that you were worthless, a nobody, a nothing. Then one day while still in that humongous room full of people where no one saw you or heard your screams, you collapsed to the floor because your mind convinced your body that it should just give up and give in. So, as you lay there unable to move, unable to speak, unable to do anything on that hard, cold floor, you grow older and older until one day because of lack of nourishment and not having the key to get yourself out of those chains, your body is then no more, and you have now turned to the dust from whence the earth bore. Everyone that is in that room continues to go about their way and even begin stepping on the dust that you have become. Until one day, someone gets tired of walking on the dust and gets a broom and a dustpan and sweeps it up, and then tosses it into the trashcan amongst all the other trash because they never knew you were even there.

They never knew you were there because your cries were masked by smiles and makeup.

They never knew you were there because your screams for help were masked by screams of laughter. They never knew you were there because your shaky arms and hands were glamorized by bracelets and rings that captured their eyes instead of the truth within you. They never knew you were there because the chains that had you bound were disguised in beautiful attire and dressed up for every occasion.

They didn't see you when you went home and cried until your eyes were red, your face was swollen, and you had no more tears left to shed. They didn't see you as you pleaded over and over again, "Why Me? Why Me?" through all the pain and agony. They didn't see you when you were on your personal ledge and at any moment anything could have come along and been the little force that was needed to push you right on over. No, not one saw you!

Yet, somehow through all of that you survived, you still have a pulse, and you still have breath. Even though no one saw you, there was a God that saw you beneath all your attempts to hide and cover up your silent cries. There was a God that heard you and rested beside you as you needed comforting. Even though no one seemed to know that you existed, there was a God, the Creator of the heavens and the Earth that knew you before you were even formed in your mother's womb and knew that you were worth it to Him.

Now, get up truth and be thine true self. Wake up spirit for the will of God is calling you. Shake off disappointment, shake off stress and depression, shake it off! Shake off anything that is not like God! You have been sleepwalking for far too long, and it is past time to awaken from REM sleep and be who and what God has called you to be. See, in the stage of REM sleep, you are dreaming. Now that you have dreamt about it, be about it. Out of my belly shall flow rivers of living water. Out of my spirit shall flow the reflection of God and His everlasting love. Now, be about God, be about your true calling! Let your true self emerge from this, whatever your "THIS" may be. There's a thing that has you sleepwalking, and you are about to walk past your destiny because you can't see; your eyes are still closed. They are covered by the eyelids of stress and depression and their friend anxiety. They are covered by the eyelids of low self-esteem and self-manipulation. Well, all of God's children hear me. Those are false eyelids that the enemy brought to you, wrapped up like some kind of gift. Well, God's children, give it back to the enemy and receive the gift God delivers.

How Do You Reach the Unreachable?

How do you reach the unreachable, the seemingly impossible task? (I must be clear; with God, all things are possible!) Yet, how do I speak to the deaf, and how do I show the blind anything that there is to either hear or see?

I asked these questions many times before and didn't get a clear resolution. As time went on and as I began to get so desperate, I knew I had to come to some conclusion about what the missing components were in order to clarify what to do and how it should be done. I knew nothing more up until this point than the day before. Our Heavenly Father spoke to my heart and said, "You must show the blind what I have shown you, and you must speak to the deaf what I have spoken to you." I asked God how to do those things. He said to do it with loving kindness. I said, "Well God, how do I show them?" and He said, "You show them just as I have, with loving kindness." I then asked the Lord, how do I speak to them? He said to speak to them just as I have, with loving kindness. I asked the Lord, what if my love isn't enough love, and what if my kindness isn't kind enough? What, O Lord, do I do to reach the unreachable? The Lord said it is my obligation to follow Him as He leads and directs. It was then that I learned that I must pray and ask for His divine will and order and follow His guidance. Seek ye first the kingdom of God, in all things, even in this. Teach me, O Lord, to love like You; even when I think I am loving, let me love like You, Jesus. Even if I think that I am kind, let my kindness be a reflection of You, O Lord, so that Your glory is magnified! When I speak, let there be the fullness of You, sweet Jesus. And in my coming and my going, let there be no traces of me, O Lord, but only evidence that You are forever present in the midst! For Your glory, O Lord! For Your glory! For Your glory!

CHAPTER 6

My Freedom

At times, it seemed so cold out, no sign of the brilliant sun. And there I was sitting and thinking about all that is and all that was, and I was feeling alone. I was filled with anxiety about what tomorrow would bring and had little hope that the change that was so desperately needed would ever come. Yet, how do you get through the exhaustion?

Have you ever been physically drained, mentally drained, or even spiritually drained? Have you ever felt them all at once? Have you ever felt like you just couldn't do anything else and that you had nothing else to give of yourself for yourself let alone anyone or anything else? Have you ever felt so tired and fatigued that all you wanted to do was sleep or not get out of bed because you weren't ready to face the day ahead and all the woes it had to offer? Have you ever felt so overwhelmed and exhausted that you wanted to throw in the towel but didn't have the strength to do it? Have you ever felt so invisible like the whole world was passing you by, and no one really sees the person you were in that moment? Have you ever screamed out, yet no one could ever hear the sound no matter how loudly you shouted, not even if you were in a room full of people? Have you been fighting from every angle, yet it seems as though you haven't moved a muscle? Have you ever cried uncontrollably that so many tears have fallen, and now your body is refusing to produce anymore? Have you ever felt like giving up on everything, but you just didn't know where to begin with the giving up process?

All that is in my world is a repetitive cycle of nonstop duties day and night with no assistance and not enough time to complete the task from the day before. I wish I had someone or something there when I was in panic mode, and my spirit felt like screaming because I was in desperate need of freedom. Each day, life brought about new tasks to add to the ones from the day before. I had become a robot, one that had feelings and got tired but kept going and couldn't stop because there was life depending on it. I couldn't let my children down no matter what. Sometimes, I couldn't even find the words to pray for myself, so all I could do was cry out and pray that God would hear my cries. If he heard me, would He understand what I meant and would He understand the nature of my distresses and how badly I needed to breathe a big, fresh sigh of relief? Please, dear Lord, deliver me! Father, help me. Father, I need You. Father, can You see me, and can You feel me? O Father, my Father, please help me. I'm being still, so I can hear You clearly. Lord, I am patiently waiting, and I just don't know what else to do…My Father is coming.

As He soothes and calms me with every gentle word felt within my heart, I am reminded a million times over that His love is never failing. Sometimes, I feel like there is no one to tell this to because I don't understand how it is that someone or anyone would ever understand what it is that I am needing to desperately convey at the depths and the magnitude at which the situational circumstances amidst me exist. The weight of carrying a heavy load of cargo all alone can be understood by many. The weight of having no one to confide in can be understood by many. The weight of going into battle with no one to help keep you covered is terrifying. I'm sure someone else can understand that. But the weight of non-existence in a world where you clearly exist, yet clearly do not is unexplainable. How do I begin to explain this to people who only know that they have always existed since birth? Maybe they can't comprehend that there is much more to become because of being in the flesh form and natural state of mind.

I once knew a little girl who had hopes and dreams of belonging somewhere. She needed it. I often spoke to her about the things that God spoke to my heart to encourage her. I told her that it was going to be okay, and God had her covered. She tried to find comfort in things that were of this world and failed to realize at those moments what she was doing. Despite it all, God kept her covered and has shown her a love far greater than anything she has ever known. Nothing could ever compare! As God beckoned her and she obeyed, things started to become clearer. This life, this world, it all belongs to God, the one who created it all and the one who is molding you and shaping you into what He needs you to be for His glory. So, whatever experiences and trials she went through brought her closer to God and closer to what He called her to be for His divine purpose.

There must be a purification that helps bring you into your true state of being, pure gold.

You must now leave the old and let the new you remain. Now that the "old you" is gone and the "new you" is left, allow God to enter in and strip away whatever is not like Him. We must stand naked before God. Jesus is our Savior, and He died on the cross, so that we would have another chance. He rose so that we would be set free and be able to enter into God's heavenly kingdom.

Another Letter to God

When my heart became so desperate and my mind was overwhelmed, thinking became unbearable. But to hear Your voice now, at this very moment, is all the peace I need. Just to be wrapped in Your living word, Father, is the very comfort and peace I need. At this moment, while writing, I am listening to such a beautiful song that my tears overflow, and my heart can't help but to leap for joy. Yes, sweet Jesus, You are my living hope! God, there is a void that needs to be filled. Correction, there are many voids to be filled in my life. Heavenly Father, You are the void filler, and You can fill every void at once. Fill these voids, dear Lord, and make me whole again. There are times when I have felt trapped, a slave of life's circumstances. The questions then arise, "Why am I not able to break free? Not able to get up and move? How do I hold it all together when I feel like I am rapidly falling apart?"

Sometimes I am just so tired of fighting and seem to get nothing accomplished. I pray and nothing seems to happen. That's when I had to learn to let God fight my battles and keep on praying because I know in due time He will answer me.

I Said Yes

When I said yes, I said yes to all of this! I said yes to the chaos that surrounds me and makes me feel like I'm slowly being consumed by it. A piece of me is being broken off little by little, and I am then left feeling empty and all alone, forgotten, and worthless.

However, when I said yes to God, this is what I said yes to. All of this. I viewed a lot of these difficult times as shortcomings and downfalls. I was in bondage to so many events that left me torn and in pieces. As my heart slowly tore away, the part that remained struggled to keep my blood flowing. In my mind, I questioned why me. I was always told that the test comes before the testimony.

Sometimes, I can't move, and I feel so helpless. I, now, realize that's what the devil wants me to be, helpless and immobile. However, the word of God says that he is a liar and the father of it. Yes, Satan is a liar! That means that the truth is the mere opposite of every negative word the enemy speaks in your ear!

I realized that I had a lot of unnecessary baggage that I had to let go of. I was holding on to my wants and desires. But when I made the decision to let go of my will and allow God to have His way and allow His will to be done in my life, that's when I felt free.

There are many times that the yearning inside goes far deeper than anything that is tangible. There may even be times when nothing seems like it is enough. I recall a time when I ate a big, delicious meal, but I still felt empty. I remember a time when I went out and bought something new and lovely, yet I still felt empty. It was at these moments that I knew something was missing from the equation. When I surrounded myself with family and friends, I still felt a void.

Have you ever had a tear fall from your eyes with no explanation? I always knew that I needed something far greater than anything I have ever known; I learned it was God's loving touch. The space that is within where greatness should reside, the emptiness within where joy should have been, only God can fill.

I say yes God, just as I did the day that You formed me in my mother's womb, and though the tears may flow, it's only this flesh because my spirit forever rejoices.

Say yes to God, then begin to embrace what is already yours!

I thank God for always being there and welcoming me with open arms! I was always His; this is the truth because He gave me life, and He has called me back to Him! For God has always loved me, even more than I have ever loved myself!

As my heart unfolded, I allowed my true self to be birthed. I am able to see and know who I am and the person that I have become for a purpose, God's purpose. Even like a faint voice within the wilderness, I was able to find the hidden gem that was buried so far beneath the surface. I had to reveal my secret struggles from somewhere deep within me in order to gain my freedom and true state of pure gold.

I pray that you are able to learn who you are and what things must be birthed through you for God's divine will and purpose to come forth in your life. I pray that the real you, the hidden gem, and your true state of pure gold is revealed and you lay down whatever secret struggles you have before the King, so you can gain your freedom.

The Eternal Candle

There is a forever burning flame that burns with the intensity of the sun, deep down within my soul, growing more and more each day. This hunger that I feel intensifies with every passing moment. Day has now turned into night, and now, the night has welcomed the day once again. Thus, the cycle continues. Whenever the sun kisses the moon, it quickly shies away and awaits the return of its distant friend from somewhere far within the Milky Way galaxy. In the midst of the darkness lies a candle, an eternal candle that ignites with the purest passions and glows whenever new life is birthed. May the light that dwells within you be a reflection of greatness that will forever shine throughout time and for all eternity.

May these words forever dwell within you…

Today I Will Be...

Today I will be who I was always
destined to be.

I will never walk alone

for the Lord, our God is forever there
guiding me.

Though the journey ahead may sometimes
seem steep,

the Lord our God will be there even as I sleep.

I know that I was created for greatness and
the love that He gives
will always show His faithfulness.

As He lights my path every step of the way, I
shall rejoice in the Lord each and every day.

All my goals, all of my dreams,
and all of my aspirations

shall all come true as I look to the Lord,
who is there pulling me through.

Today, I will be who I was always
destined to be,

and I say thank You, Jesus, for never
letting go of me.

This is just a part of my story, a part of my journey, and a few moments in time... Embrace the
greatness that lives within and let it help guide
you through life's journey in leaving an infinite
lasting impression that signifies your legacy.

About the Author

Glinda L. Brock resides in Manning, South Carolina. Her mission is to uplift, inspire, and motivate others within her community and around the world to discover and ignite the greatness hidden within them. She volunteers as chair of the Student Improvement Council at the local high school and as vice chair of the same organization at the junior high school.

Glinda is passionate about being a beacon of light who reflects greatness while helping others and spreading love. Her desire is to be a true reflection of extraordinary purpose, leaving an everlasting imprint that can light the path for the people she encounters now and in future generations. She is inspired to share her own struggles and stories with others in hopes that they will find strength in her experiences.

Her hobbies include spending time with her family and friends, traveling, baking, arts and crafts, writing, and participating in a host of outdoor activities. She has two amazing sons, Amarion and Nehemiah.

To connect, email glinda.brock@yahoo.com

CREATING DISTINCTIVE BOOKS
WITH INTENTIONAL RESULTS

We're a collaborative group of creative masterminds
with a mission to produce high-quality books to position
you for monumental success in the marketplace.

Our professional team of writers, editors, designers,
and marketing strategists work closely together to ensure
that every detail of your book is a clear representation
of the message in your writing.

Want to know more?
Write to us at info@publishyourgift.com
or call (888) 949-6228

Discover great books, exclusive offers, and more at
www.PublishYourGift.com

Connect with us on social media

@publishyourgift

CPSIA information can be obtained
at www.ICGtesting.com
Printed in the USA
LVHW081637040122
707840LV00012B/283